Insomn

James Waller (b.1978) is an Australian born artist and poet of mixed Maltese, English and Irish ancestry. He studied Visual Arts at Sydney College of the Arts, Newcastle University and the Malmo Art Academy, and Art History at the University of Melbourne. He has been a featured poet in numerous events in Melbourne, Brisbane and Dublin, including Passionate Tongues, The Dan Poetry readings, The Courthouse readings, The Spinning Room (Melbourne), Speed Poets (Brisbane), Brown Bread Mix Tape (Dublin) and the Clonakilty Arts Festival (Clonakilty, Ireland).

A full time artist and writer, he lives in Clonakilty, Ireland, where he runs the Clonakilty School of Painting, teaching classical painting, drawing and printmaking to children and adults. *Insomnia's Gates* collates his first three collections of poetry written in the Summer and Autumn of 2005. For more of his work visit: www.jameswaller.org

Nicholas Powell is an Australian poet, author of Water Mirrors (2012) and Trap Landscape (forthcoming 2021). He lives in Finland.

Insomnia's Gates

James Waller

Poems

First published 2021
© James Waller (poems), 2021
© Nicholas Powell (Introduction), 2021

ISBN: 9798711002925
Imprint: Independently published
Typeset in Baskerville 11 & 14pt

This book is copyright. Aside from fair dealing for the purposes of study, criticism, review, or as otherwise permitted under the Copyright Act, no part may be reproduced by any process without written permission. Inquiries should be addressed to the publisher.

Cover image: *Dulle Griet*, by Pieter Breughel (1563)
Located in the Museum Mayer van den Bergh, Antwerp.
Image and file are in the Public Domain.

Cover concept and design: James Waller
Layout editor: Sheila Mullins

Acknowledgements

Surrender first appeared in the second edition of Page Seventeen. Many of these poems have been read at poetry gigs in Melbourne, Dublin and Clonakilty. A big thank you to the conveners and to the vibrant poetry community in Melbourne, which provided the first space for these poems to emerge. Special thanks to Nicholas Powell for his generous feedback and for introducing this volume, and to Sheila for her love and counsel.

Contents

Introduction   IX
by Nicholas Powell

I. Burning Stones

Mistress of News	3
Baron	5
Muse	6
Autumn Wine	7
Heat	9
The Gift	10
Wedding Feast	12
Doubt	14
For Jennifer	15
Haze	16
Burning stones	17
Child of the Hunt	18
Etching in the Granite	19
Morning	20
Nanna's Age	21
Sequestration	22
Song of the Tavil	23
Impotence	24
Witness	25
Sunday	27
Milosz's Sail	29
Bicycle Song	30
Rembrandt's Eyes	32
Puppetry	33
Glazes on the Highway	35
Prayer	37
Beloved	39
The Master	41
The Tower of Language	43
Sleep	44

Night Song	45
Travel	46
Remonstration	48
Chambers of Autumn Fire	49
Quavers	51
Criminal Music	52
Family of Soil	53
Dust	54
Across the Salt Pan	56
Shadows on the Ground	57
The Painter	58
The Music	59
Tables of Wine	61
Dear Patrick	62
Tunji and Fernando	63
The Magic Cat is Singing	64

II. Rings of Blue

Uncovered	67
Gentle Blue	68
Offering	70
Beads	71
Rings of Blue	72
Surrender	73
Child	74
Icon	75
Ascension	76
Faithless	77
For Ania	78
Rinsed in Night	79
For Osip	80
Akhmatova's Eyes	81
Anna's Song	82
Shadows	83
Migration	84
Donkey	85
Bach	86

Patrick's Hand	87
Invitation	88
Standing	89
Pastoral	90
Cheek	91
Dreams	92
Still and Washed	93
The Path	94
Harvest of Suns	95
The Pieces Fall	96
Arrangement	97
Promise	98
Blue Fire	99
Ageless Songs	100
The Blue Universe	101
The Endless Suns	102
Cold	103
Kiefer's Song	104
Reflections	105
Caress	106
The Black Dog	107
Where is the Hammock?	108
Tale of the Hammock	109
Fists of Now	110

III. Blinded Bulls

The Tree of Alchemy	113
A Rain of Blood	114
Blinded Bulls	115
The Dogs of Midnight	116
Thunder	117
Minotaur	118
Nocturne	119
Insomniacs of Nature	120
Pale Thunder	121
On Picasso	122
Gold Rain	123

Land Mines	124
Oppenheimer's Score	125
Days Eternal	126
Warning	127
Monstrous Wire	128
Untouched	129
Songs Unfathomable	130
Lorca's Guitar	131
Shield	132
Blinded Lethe	133
Ships	134
Gone	135
Albatross	136
Gilding	137
Pale Gold	138
Wealth	139
Growth	140
Vision	141
Promises	142
In the Libraries of Night	143
Lethe's Shadow	144
Tips of Fire	145
Tales of the Mirror	146
Poor Lethe	153
Notes on the Poems	155
Recurring Motifs and Symbols	166

Illustrations *(by the author)*

Fork-Hand (charcoal 2005)	1
Archangel, after Giotto (lino 2021)	65
Minotaur and Child (lino, 2021)	111

Introduction

Entering Insomnia's Gates, we find ourselves in the painter's studio - "thud of a dropped palette", "a fantasy hovering in the canvas of space". Throughout this tripartite collection, paint and voice coalesce, manifesting the tensions and parallels between sibling mediums.

Waller's exquisitely weighted lines have a precise and spry musicality that never jars. The integration and accretion of image and sound, informed by a physicality of thought, lead to moments of astonishment that are not infrequent. These poems bear repeated readings. Elegiac and epistolary, they address friends and artistic influences, and travel from the local and temporal to foreign, less secular realms of the imagination, where language enacts psychic frottage on exigent matters of vital force. The impression is sincere and other-worldly.

Elemental motifs glow and shadow: bronze, gold, heat, wings, the organic and the mineral. *Chambers of Autumn Fire* offers homage to Milosz, Akhmatova, Mandelstam, and Celan, echoes of whom are to be discerned throughout, poets of witness and the large gesture. Not inhibited or constrained by poetry à la mode, Waller's debt is to the voices and canvases of Europe, to examples of committed artistic integrity under conditions of great pressure.

Despite their European antecedents, these are poems of place, in particular Melbourne, albeit transfigured. Hear "the screeching banshee of Fitzroy Street /Ascends and descends /In its eternal round/ Of Mechanical Hell". Waller does not forego the mundane in favour of the numinous; rather, the numinous is quotidian, and vice versa. Note that the spirit is ecumenical, in no way preachy.

In the superb poem, *The Magic Cat is Singing*, "anonymous fires wander insatiably" until "Water drops / With slow dramatic intensity". Rain is palliative, but there is a further dénouement: "Hidden in the castle / Cats are playing / With Balthus' ball of colour". Earlier, the speaker asks: "Music, must I hold your cup forever?" a question to which the ball of colour comes as an apt rejoinder. With deceptive simplicity, the opening lines of *Gentle Blue* evoke opulent possibility: "I am awake / I am asleep / Paper is a child/ And wire is a song". Unadorned metaphor morphs the artist's materials into symbols of innocent complexity.

Painterly is a too-easy descriptor for these poems, which, for all their surface texture, have a larger ambition— to access areas of inner experience that are often occluded in lyric poetry. With astonished curiosity and sentiment tempered by history, each part of this trilogy is born of necessity. Rings of Blue is in dialogue with the artist's installation works featuring blue neon rings, as well as icons. As in the proverbial grain of sand, the speaker finds a world within beads: emerald, vermillion, cerulean shades, chains of colour manifest as fruits in the hand are "the growing castle/ Gathering in my beads". It is utterly tactile work that exudes the palpable temperature of things in themselves, but also what they stand for in Waller's symbolic, but never gnomic, poetic.

Waller says he thinks of art as the "incantation of an arcane force, speaking itself into being, raising itself through emotional bodies of myth and symbol, in arrangements wholly other, wholly strange, wholly true." As such, this poetry is best taken on its own terms. Its version of radical subjectivity is baroque-romantic; never cynical, save in passing contempt for military-industrial chicanery circa 2003. There's also a cheeky quasi-haiku, and a pair of typographic pattern-poems.

Blinded Bulls resounds with *Oppenheimer's Score*. Lorca's lost guitar is found by the roadside. The Minotaur too, is lost, led by the wounded child through a "sadist century". The poet's gaze is fierce yet gentle, finding solace where it can in a violent wilderness.

Insomnia's Gates coheres around fluid forms of lineation, pace and space. Formal elements resolve the paradox of how to make the arcane accessible, reaching for Chopin's gold standard - simplicity as the final achievement. To that end, generous end-notes are illuminative. The reader is free, however, to take Marianne Moore's advice and "take probity on faith and disregard the notes".

Being self-published does not diminish the many admirable qualities of this book. It is perhaps inevitable that such an uncompromising voice turns away from the sentries of verse, and enters through gates of its own design.

Nicholas Powell,
January 2021, Helsinki

*for all those who need their hands cooled
and for my teachers
who showed me the fire*

I
Burning Stones

Mistress of News

Calico curtains billow in the tower
Bringing news of hot wind
And Summer's hand
The studio is kept cool by outer bricks
Baking in the sun

The lake of the present shifts its gaze
Around trembling waters.
Far away – disturbances,
Below, the shish and thud of a dropped palette

Vibrations of fridges talk to the air
And, via radio, statistics of death climb
In pursuit of a higher score.

The universe seems idle
And radio statistics not quite believable.
Indeed belief melts away in
Brunswick Street's hedonistic air

My thanks to the creative beggar
And the weak yellow-toothed grin-
Ships of poverty loosed from the harbours of self.
The screeching banshee of Fitzroy Street
Ascends and descends
In its eternal round
Of Mechanical Hell
If we turn the radio off the news is still bad
And as we walk noises lay hidden –

The mistress of news billows the curtain
She has arrived dripping with light,
Her back is burning
And her eyes are hollow.
Do not be afraid Son of Dream
Reality has both cursed and blessed your kin

At this Ian's tenor rises in song
In unison with the screams of a child

The mistress has left and I am faced
With a cloud of gold -
A fantasy hovering in the canvas of space.
Music flares and my body remembers
The distant ships of composition -
Veins of power scorched in the Invisible.

They are the songs and screams of children,
The songs and silences of adulthood.

Baron

A reign of quiet heat claims the hillside
Whilst the farmers play darts in the cool
February is the Monarch of the hour
As we hear attempts to strip a baron
Of his title - far away
Where games are more deadly
And things smaller than darts
Fly with random hate
Breaking songs of insurgence in mid air.
But that has no consequence here.
A beer is drained of its amber life
And the midday pub is as quiet as a
Whispered *Terra Australis*

Muse

My burning mistress has faded into the blackened gloom
The music evades my hands
And threatens to engulf
The stability of Reason
O Muse of Fire, unquenchable
Take another's hand
Leave mine for songs of enchanted calm
So we pray, artists thrown upon the coals,
Eyes in the beam of Heaven's reproach
With voices we grab beams of silence
And twist them into words
Trees are golden in Autumn
And charred after the fire
The earth dances upon and through us all
The curtain rips in the wind
And the chasm remains open

Autumn Wine

I

The Mistress dances in the trees
The fires of summer have cooled
And a slow mantle settles upon the streets
Memory broadens
In the aftermath of her havoc;
Illicit Dreamer, drunkard of the fog
Where were you when he ripped out his soul
And cast away his hopes?

II

The wine bottle rang
A voice from the dark;
The news was ill
And a spectre emerged with words of chaos
Which tangled in the room
That was summer, this is autumn
That was the north, this is the south
But memory ripens unexpectedly
Where are you now illicit dreamer,
Drunkard of the fog?

III

Banished from memory
Music runs now like a river
Songs from the Mistress' mottled fingers
Is that blood on her leaves? Wine?
Or veins of happiness
Which course through her trembling being?

IV

The arcades of autumn have awoken
Desire wanders through tippled humanity
And sighs flow from his anonymous light.

Heat

Our old house allowed every breeze through its walls-
All was breath and crackling fire,
The snapping of twigs and the gathering of wood.
I lit the fire and warmth spread in the room-
A warmth rising and falling, dwindling and cooling,
I shared a room with my brother there-
We camped inside its walls-
Within its dark strangeness I discovered
An uncontrollable heat.
It mingled with the darkness and festooned
Into the rituals of night
It played into the future;
A harpsichord of nocturnal song
Praising dams, soft earth
And the bicycle tracks of youth.

The heat grew and flared in the hands of early discoveries
Was then caught in funereal stillness
Where it raged in secret, unknown to the world
The power of the Beast is great
And containment is a lost art
But for a gift which arrived on nocturnal wings

Like solar wind the fire flared once more
Escaping the gift
And ravaging space.
Curse the hands of power
Bless the hands of song
Pray for the eternal wisdom of the gift
Only it may save us from the prophecies
Of the ancient hearth
And the wilderness of unearthly memories.

The Gift

An abandoned telegraph pole stands still in the dam
An egret is perched upon its worn battlement
The water level has dropped
From water bombing I am told.
We pray for rain
And chant the psalms to a Hebrew god,
In words which remember blood and sacrifice,
In words which echo the terror
Of children in a holy, unholy city
Solomon's wisdom cannot heal Jerusalem

The chant calms and centres the mind
Like the egret it is perched in fluttering stillness
Arcadia holds the power of solitude,
Its rustling habits the keys to silence
On a hillside the heart is groomed
Like a horse
To cantor in the sun

Gabriel surrendered long ago
On a journey through Italian hills
He knows who is the Drawer
And who is the Drawn
Like Rumi knew

Eighty years for blushing Gabriel

A brother of strength,
He sees The Gift.
At first light before the bell
In cherished silence
A psalm is sung.

Forgive me, I am weak
There are too many paths,
All are lined with fire
And Jerusalem rings in contradiction to my heart.

Doubt

Tape rips and trolleys trundle
Louvres rattle in the wind
The day is overcast -
Summer tempered by
The cold hands of the south.

I have lost touch with time,
An indecent scrawl covers the wall
And doubts hunger and crowd
Like Kurasawa's demons.

The solution forms a wall against the ink
For thoughts to be revealed.
She arcs in a mythical breeze,
A wax idol
For a fevered hand.
She arcs and grows
Under Pygmallion's gaze,
Takes life
And shudders with breath.
Better to be wax
Better to be ink
But for the glint
In the coin of the eye
Which wanders into a distant music...

A white powder stains the pan,
Algae blooms in the solution.
What mad fate has decreed
This rush of impotent waves?
Fantasy blooms with the algae
Not one stroke is real
Kurasawa's demons haunt me
They whisper all day long

For Jennifer

Fresh flowers on a mound of earth
Thomas street is quiet
Cars line the road and fill the drive
It is not Sunday and the Anglican church is empty
Rain pours and we run
Freedom frightens the air
Departure assaults the tendons of life
Which are wracked with suppressed pain
Why is forbidden
There is no why
Only earth, sunglasses on a cloudy day
And endless photographs
Which fan the fires of January
All through the wastelands of loss
No fire is deliberately lit
That is a lie
Ask our mothers, they know
The sun sparks grief
And the plains are scorched
With disappearance.

Haze

The haze has grown
It thickens in a speech of freedom
"We will spread democracy"
Yes, like typhus it will spread
Like a widening pool of blood under
The head of a child
The haze has grown and we dare not go out
The frightened air of January is darkening the sky
The Reverend speaks of acts of God
Fool! The earth is, we are
And the actions of earth
Are the blades of our human growth
If you like, God shall wander as fire
Or as wave, or as the thunder
Of the shifting earth
It matters not to the haze which chokes,
The hot fluids which sing.
A geological pageant is afoot
A gown which swirls amidst the stars
Ask the unknown child,
The invisible friend hidden in the cloak of war
Goya's Collossus strides still,
Picasso's Guernica wrestles on,
Saint John's head flies in the Feast Of Venus -
As nations depart from the struggle
The stars and stripes whip
With ever greater force
The haze grows and grows
Visibility is almost nill.

Burning Stones

Burning stones
Heat Summer's hand
The creek is cool
It claims our limbs
In a slow sultry embrace
Naked we climb to the pulse
Of the ageless bush
Naked we dream in fantasies
Of Forever
A tick of a thistle and scratching in the sun
A bridge lies overhead
But cries are quickly absorbed
You wade behind
A goddess of discovery
Together we reach the spring of desire
Effulgent in Debussy's phrasing
Delicate as a hymn in a distant monastery
You believe in God
So do I
But I also believe in stones
They are phrases which burn in the cool creek
Phrases which never lose your scent.

Morning

Footsteps govern the floorboards
Time has retreated
Into those who bother
The tea is warm and cascades through the body
Light glares through the clouds
Cars remonstrate with the noises
Of the night before
Cartwheels of laughter which arced through the gloom
Feathering drunken lamps with ritual forgetting
Defying the mortal screen with amber
Chasing breathless desire
With heartbeats hidden
Under tables stuck to dreams
As a pan crackles
And eggs awaken from their shells

Nanna's Age

Nanna's age reflects families
Which cluster the wall
I am there somewhere
A faithless hand with reconciling eyes
Mother's travels spread over the earth
My eyes are hers
And travel beyond
Where families shine in the deep
Fantasies sifted in the gold digger's pan
Pyrite glints under the clothesline
The bush is the flavour of heat
We must pass the ring of sulphur
Follow the great pipeline
White as an English water serpent
To the sea
Untold flowers bloom along the way
Water tanks rise as
Corrugated towers in the desert
The caravan shivers in the night
Where we are going names drift
Fires recede
And poetry dances in the future.

Sequestration

Like a gypsy in a motionless caravan
I play an invisible guitar
Sounds are erupting from the centre
And hands turn into speeches of gold
Which are cast into blackened limbs
With plaster ground from the earth
Ground from the white bones
Of lives which swayed in the heat
Which sway in the tracts
Of the crackling bush
Anniversaries of song pulse in the sky
With wings of numberless return
Sheets of power billow in the sun
Off clotheslines rammed into the earth
Pain rises in geological fissures
We have dug too deep
And now madly plan to refill
Sequestration forms four chords
Of horror under the crust
And basins tremble with the insane
Wisdom of the few
These chords are blackened
Gold is for another age
If only paper could whisper reason
But history shows that is futile
The earth's arm is stretched
And the needle is poised.

Song of the Tavil

Dadadim Dadada Dadadim Dadim Dadim Dada Dadadim Da Da Dadim Dadim Da Da Dim Dada Dadadim Dadim Dim Dada Dim Dim Dim Dada Dadim
Hand vibrations flood the taut skin
Black curls sway behind closed eyes
Shifting position in a gradual rise
And an interminable fall
Dark veins gleam as a doorway forms
Vibrations echo and die in a sensory rod
And reform in the fingers which leap
And sense the coming speed in
The ageless spirit of the tavil
Which haunts the hands
And rises to take hold
In trembling staccatto cries
Which only just hold on
To the perspiration of reason
And the strangeness of the crowd
Astonished we are held with the artist
For one moment
In limbo
For one moment we face the door
How can we know that door?
Why are we drawn?
By what invitation?
The hands recover
And the collective breath subsides
We will be drawn back
To whichever veil
Without knowledge
But with dance enflaming our limbs.

Impotence

You who stained Akhmatova's hands
With the blood of a witness
You who prosper from death
I have marked you in the book from the beginning
Polished teak will not resist
The hammer blows when the sun falls
Golden rings will wish
They had never seen the light
As the temperature soars
The streets become still
Paris and Madrid are emptied in their annual exodus
I pray this fountain would grow
And ease the collective burden
But ink is nothing
Besides dark fountains which rise
And scorch the air with pain
And cover the countryside
With black tears of ash
Mingled with rain
A bird picks at some fruit
Pigeons wander across the granite
And the pen darts with a surge of life
A script of haze which limns the fog
A script of impotent fury

Witness

Dogs are standing motionless in the square
Imagined monuments to my brother's hunt
Children are playing in giddy circles
Besides mothers who converse with arms folded
Somewhere a siren wails
And heated bitumen undulates through the city streets
Grass is an anonymous saint amongst
Heathen roads
Which lead to themselves
In the mischief of urban antics
An ever present rumble pervades the ground
Trolleys rattle with silver tempers
Mothers' hands snap with the bites of the young
And electric oaths stream in the metallic sun
Papers fly over the wide haze
Full of news which smudges
On idle uncaring thumbs
Bus loads of passengers who cannot wait
To be elsewhere sigh against the windows
Elsewhere news smudges into smoke
The acrid tip which burns
And glances with a greedy eye
At every fluttering strip
Strips which curl in abject surrender
Like thistles under the hammer
Of the January fire
A city dissembled with unrolled bills
Parts its hair at the gambling till
Swollen eyes in the morning light
Take destitute steps
Through a park strewn with waste
O city of unrelenting consumate haste!

Garbage trundles and clangs in the early hours
Before night which colluded in nocturnal rites
Night which shone with an ardent torch
Air tastes the flames of industry's fountain
An Olympian light which grows and sears
Marking no athlete's star touched rise
But smouldering in witness
To the dark and impenetrable
Years
Of a century blinded by fire

Don't worry Nadia
The fire in your limbs is greater
The spirit which glints in your eye
More powerful than a thousand suns
Dance sweet one and dispel these dark dreams!

Sunday

Fitzroy rains guitars this Sunday
And musicians appear all around
With boxes under their arms
And smiles which promise
The music of days to come.
Lightheaded the ground disappears,
Coffee swirls and clinks
And laughter grazes the asphalt.
Tired chords are blooming in the sun
And everywhere hearts of fancy glide
Upon a solar river
Leading to the playful One.
Games grow into the evening
Whilst prayers are offered
Under the ceiling of Saint Patrick's
The young pray in amber ale
And forsake the stillness of a Mighty God
Everyone is climbing in liquid
To the sounds of distant lyres
Greek myths which glance off sunglasses
And burn in the embrace of night
A night in which Pan chuckles, mischief whistles
And the froth of future dawns escapes.
I am searching for the ground
What happened to the ground?
It is late and my head is aching.

Milosz's Sail

Stories whip across the streets
And Bach unravels in a river of notes
Timed into lasting atoms
Painting awaits
Mystery aches in my hand
Milosz is a tome of jewels
Heavy with the scarred ruins of those
He knew and those he didn't know
A brace of life which accepts illusions of forms
In exchange for the slim consolations of music
Fractures of light which stain the ground
With echoes of a paradise lost
Milosz is our Polish sail
Who never forgets or misses
Those moments of time
Which reform the atomic structure of things
Those moments which charge vision and space
Before others realize the new steps
His sails are taut
And teach our young rigging
How to observe carefully the tale in an eye
The wound in a glance
And the shifting schemes of those
Drunk with power
Who dandle the babes of lives
Arrogantly in their laps.
Stories whip and the pulse gathers strength
Bach is unceasing as the unremitting call
Of the ageless and deep
Necessity
Of music's singed and sobbing wing.

Script is as light as a butcher's knife
And truth is a laughing fire.
Stories whip and lunge
Like dogs in a playful game
The solar river is wide
And humanity basks in its breathing.
To the children of a new century
Comes the mantle
Of Milosz's eyes
The atomic notes of Bach
And a blue feather for an unwritten page.

Bicycle Song

The bicycle sings in the wind
A flight of revolving love
For a day blessed
In a sun bitten city
Along a creek
Which remembers the earth
Which follows the clouds of midges
And ducks and weaves with the flight of birds
Which dart and chase in the underbrush
Young gums appear in focus
With a gentle shock of presence
The wind recedes
The rush of the ride seeps away
And stillness gradually invades my limbs
Quiet broadens in a loose woodland
Awaiting with eternal calm
The sun's slow descent
In anticipation of a cool glow
Which forms like gems that lay hidden
In the shadows of the hills of Moonbi
A village far to the north
Where my mother ponders the evening
And my brother stalks his prey
Further north my sister's thoughts are hidden
And over the sea my father survives his demons
He heaves with a heart which yearns for love
Paradise in a golden shower
Sometimes shields a tragic harvest
Night is here and sculptures stand in the lamplight

Paints promise colour in the darkness
And songs walk with emerald eyes
Throughout a city young and tempting
With reigning curves of beauty.
A friend calls in a voice which quavers
Like a distant ghost
I am harsh
We were brothers
Who walked together in the moonlight
The moonlight which always shines
On faces lost from sight
On bonds broken and bonds reformed
Like lunar clouds that hide
And in hope
Re-reveal the spirit.
Sunday rests in blue neon
The bicycle will sing again
In a day ardent with the power which lifts.

Rembrandt's Eyes

Sleep escapes the hunter of flame
My arm aches with mystery's code
An arm which revels
In Mandalstam's gold
And awakens the terror and life
Hidden in the wings of pastel
And the pliant gift of wax
Figures walk with moonlight gait
Through the lamplit hour
Black forks blaze in a shimmer of life
And the hunter's prey rears with a flash of strength
Hounds are loosed in wire and foam
Alsations fight in soundless rings
Memories of country walks and earthly things
Bay in these restless wanderings
Seeking the surface
Are the forms of life
To be freed
In the intoxicating majesty of space
The hinterland of trembling art
Breathing truth like steam
From the flaring nostrils of morning
In winter's chill dewed pasture
A race has begun
To cure the blindness
To be drawn
To be ascended
To be saved from the ravaging dogs of time
To hold the spear of life
Flooded with the tears which gather
In Rembrandt's eyes.

Puppetry

The clouds are heavy and low
Red light reflects from the apartments
For sale across the street
A mauve glare hides the sky
And the banshee screeches
Its mechanical good morning
Tea, garlic, and a silver fork
Are all that's needed for a life in stillness
The tied calico rests
And the streets hum in their gradual rise
Like a puppet drowned and re emerging
In the sun
Which must remember through the drowsy haze
The promise it gave in the wonderland of birth
True it wasn't asked for
But remonstrating with one's existence
Is a futile exercise
Which invites the laughter of demons
And other things of shadow
No the coil must rise
Like a deadly cobra to a magical pipe
We do not have such daily compressions here
That sway in India's consciousness
Perhaps a crocodile man in every square?
The economy is booming so cobras and crocodiles
Can disappear
Along with artists and our indigenous brethren
Who, inspite of the latest musicals on classic FM
Still wander the streets in the misery of loose change.

Carol, I hope that you have found
The change of the present which creates the future
Frank, I pray the demons won't last forever
And Jack, whose white bearded Shakespearean
Tower of voice has pounded the theatre stage,
I pray these latter years will give you respite
From your ravaged wanderings.

The trimble is hushed
As a tradesman walks the roofs
Protecting us from clouds
Which lay heavy on a Melbourne morning.

Glazes on the Highway

Glazes on the highway of washed out rain
Fields drunk in the stupor of canola yellow
Songs are played on a worn out tape
And the country glides with ever turning eyes
We sing in the exulted morning
To cows with slow jaws
And horses which prance in cautious curiosity
Robert glints in the bush with the laughter of Pan
A fire of joy along an eroding creek bed
The hill is a castle of ancient friends
Which dream evening into their limbs
The eternal evening which beckons showers and hail
Frost and sun burnt offerings
The walls are lined with inflections of
The outer realm
Bathed in deep crimson hues
Which tie in an unknown chord
To the flight of an inner impulse
Which darts and scrubs
In a fever of life
Hot soup warms the body
An open door befriends the night
Trains tremble by with nameless haste
Carrying futile pillows and sleepless eyes
In a rhythm of mechanical hum
Birds of night sail in remembrance
Of deathless chimes in forgotten cities
Hidden by dust
Razed by fire
And bombed in the choking speech of war -

Fly away birds
But your wings are broken;
This century breaks my heart
With its senseless hate.

Brushed with canola yellow
In the wide world of light brimmed pastures
Young lambs chase and play
Like domestic pups
And children who chase in circles
With the birds.

Prayer

We drove forever
Through endless scrub
Upon sun warmed trails
Which fought the pounding sky
With surging crust
The hand on the wheel
Was blessed with a love of earth
With the joy of song which opened the banjo
Into the dry western air
We drove on passed sleep
Into mud swirled memory
Awake with the interminable hum of vast distances
And incalculable stretches of blue
Trees swayed in the dark
Upon a mountain mysterious
Figures silhouetted in the eye of a truck window
In the early hours of morning
My father I remember everything
The donkey
The coals of dying fires
Silences unceasing
And jokes which frolicked with abandon
All the more painful to feel the whip
Which cracked inside of you
O I would love to strangle that demon
And release your soul of compassion
For the trembling earth
To reunite our kin
In the blood which whispers from birth

But you are far away
And the chasm is deep
Take flight letters of gold
Find the desperate song
Which is doubled over in pain
And lift it above the earth
Where in freedom it can sing
With banjo strings made taut by your son.

Beloved

Shadows were absolved in our meeting,
Light sung in our hands
It was both a joy and a challenge to be with you.
You who planted a forest
Whilst your country fell apart
You who balanced a rock spinning above your head.
You have DaVinci eyes,
Beautiful and fierce,
A mind of courageous power
Which would split the hideous face
Of Terror's loosed hound.
What joy breathes in your limbs
With a carriage not unlike
Akhmatova's somnolent poise.
The waters have separated our lives
And I know these lines
Would cause you to blush
As you whisper to your sleepy child to hush
But song, as you know, breaks
Like an ice berg from the arctic
And there is no arguing
With geological hymns
Which grow in your fiery eyes
Which leap like bolts of colour
Across black paper
And singe the clay through your hands
Into a tragic mandolin and the breath of Red Silver.
At night I look for our meeting
In the lands of forever
Where the corporeal has blended
With the immaterial stars

But better to be held in friendship's wings,
In earth's sure harness
And to build a bridge across the divide
So our spirits may hunt in a ringing of spears
To catch fresh light
For the love of those unborn,
For Theadora's dance
And the new steps
Of our century's growth.

The Master

The days have blurred in the revolving Banshee's pitch
How I wish they would oil that door!
Sounds are nailing my fingers
To a tune
Reserved for a witness.

How many lives are sailing in this wondrous hour?
How many curtains are ripping in summer's draft?
And as for those without curtains
Exposure is a necessary craft.

A child screams below as trolleys trundle,
Naked beams of silver flash with discordance
Upon the road.
The evening is long
And the golden blue air
Sits with seamless translucence
Upon a silhouette of bars.

The gathering night is staked
With a breathless pageant
Flowing in the atmosphere;
Birds dart and drop
From the signal towers
And window pains reveal stains of dried water,
Forming memories
Of a studio to the north
Where light glowed as if in another time,
Passing through castles of colour
Founded by a King of Space.

Adam and Eve watched over me there
Through nights held in history's pause.
Dust befitted the long glance of a mystery
Which filled the century's hours
With a dancing depth,
Which touched an un namable expanse.
I was suspended and am suspended still
In that bewitching junction
That intimated feasts on the brink of nowhere.

My shield of colours gave birth in a case of gold,
Upon the bench of a master
Who ascended from birth to death
In the offspring of a syntax
Measured by its embrace of nature's arc
And the prehistory of the spirit
Which flooded its ruins with the river of the hunt -

Hands of water holding spears of grace
And casting them into eternity.

The Tower of Language

It is late and the floors are marching
With staccatto steps above
I am in love with an island
Found in the limitless sea of words
A broom punctuates the floorboard ballet
As the stereo relays
Music from other times
Words climb like towers
Of boyhood coins
Which were saved in the event
Of our family becoming poor
What a curious child!
Invisible, the towers are growing
And gathering into rings of glinting silver
Upon the shores of language
Mother, they will not fund the holiday
About which we always talk
But they have formed and are forming a passage
Of laws to graze with tender knowing
Our paths sombre, bitter, lost, found
Our paths of struggle, loneliness, despair,
Our paths of tears and laughter,
Of departure between our lives
This, our island, is no holiday destination
But a bridge in the deep
A gift which may hold you aloft
Like the wings of your prayers
Which have consoled you
In your grief.

Sleep

From the eye of the silent dog
In the mythical square
Come notes which are marching
And waves of impotent fury
Engulfing my hand
With songs that are swarming
Like Liam's beehive
Twice thrice in one day
Serge kisses his cats and
Murmurs wisdom to the air
Dogs are fighting beyond the sea
Sleep walks away
And wanders to Arcadia
Where the dam water rises
And gives strength to Mario's garden
Our brother with an invisible wound
Who with joy finds treasures
Of spuds in the ground
The tables sit with ageless simplicity
In a quiet room
Gabriel shifts his chair
And Bernard closes his eyes
The deep peace of his closed eyes
In an age savaged by cuff linked beasts
Bless the Brothers of Saint Benedict's
Bless Serge and Judy in their home
The silent dog is sniffing cars of poison
And rust which cracks
In the hot nights of summer.
Sleep has returned
And the dog is still.

Night Song

There is a pageant of sounds
Masquerading in the dark
A castle of script feeding on the air
And sounds which labour for birth
Float across the battlements
Night compressions sink beyond memory
And a fairy tale city lines my astonished vision
Words are hammering
Upon society's outer limbs
As women in scared muslin
Lower their gazes to the ground
Like planes retouching a friendly port
A muffled television blares
The night snakes out
And a foot steps
With a haze of bright stars
And fire tainted whispers
Which lean into my ear.

Travel

Strength returns in the computer's glare
And the fan whirs in a favourable speech
The night drifted with mysterious suns
And a distant city in Russia's south
Which in a play of pure fantasy
Conjured Saint Basil's fairy tale spires
Travel is a beating heart
Which plays through our limbs in a heady rush
Cambodia or Tibet?
The princess questions her court
Regarding her annual flight
The face of travel's hidden God
Flares in tumbling ink
And warnings march across the screens
Of Flight Centres' answers
The question of numbers
Is the description of an age
When time's seamless strength
Has become the incest of weakened years
Somewhere in the world
Cully's fiery locks
Are swinging in a reunion of the spirit
In Mexico Gustavo strokes charcoal into a deepening breath
No longer corpses but fearless Buddhas
Emerge from his hand
From the enlightenment of
Travel's
Unexpected paths.
Come into the cool river
There is a furnace growing outside -

Inside the journeys are free
Within the studio walls
I am lying on Norway's shores
On Finland's ships
Which pass anonymous islands in the dark
Stars on the tips of seas
Wash unknown light upon eyes of wonder
Gradually dreams will fade
To re-emerge in physical departure
The studio door will close
And a sign shall read:
Travelling.

Remonstration

Like a child who wants to play
With his ill and shivering dog
You take Bacon's smearing pinks and reds
And plant a pot of flowers.
Are you an adult or are you a child?

The gypsy's invisible guitar
Is life's invitation
And the smoke which grows
From the blackening hand
Is a haze of immaterial fury -

Strip yourself down
Stand naked in the sun
And feel the heat
Which bites deep
Into Summer

Chambers of Autumn Fire

Temples dwell in the distance of my eye
With unfaltering steps the leaves bow down
In honour of your hidden glory
Stories have grown in the temple's trees
And glisten like red grapes in the sun
Autumn's chambers of fire
Play like invisible vertebrae
To a secret posthumous score
Of Vivaldi's and Cohen's violins combined.

Deep in the heart
With an immaterial ray
I am scorched with the breathing of suns
Whose light fractures in Milosz's house
In the solemn cinder of Akhmatova's voice
In the aural wave of Mandelstam's hand
And the ashen spells of Paul Celan

O chambers of autumn fire!
Your kingdom burns
In Rumi's quest
In the wings of Farīd 'Din Attar's birds
Mine is the hand of a furnace
Which sobs in terror before your gate
Where black dogs howl
And all is still

Take heart Friend
The spear is a limb of life
The fire is a curtain which may tear
In the light of love renewed

And if we are prepared, if we are strong
We may dance with the young
In the reflection of this splendour
Which streams in the Northern skies
Which glints in Balthus' paints
And which charges with life
The flaming rocks of the Australian bush -

Formed in pale lichen the sphinx of Moonbi sits
In a bed of granite
As a witness and a guard
To this cathedral of the stars.

Quavers

Quavers of space give ordinance
To the structure of thoughts
Thoughts bind the elements
And assemble rings of birds
A coalesced composition which scatters
In the following movement:

A grey eyed pianist
Sits with a swan arced neck
A finger poised above a key -

Thirty seconds of sun parched summer
Dries the mouth in expectation;
Throw a stone in a river
Cool the hands of music
Abandon all care in a wondrous hammock!

The pianist sits still as the water ripples

Croque Monsieur loosens his classical bonds
With bows which quiver
(Against the quavers)
With mischievous haste
Above the bar
Under the lights
In a haze of smoke.

Criminal Music

Blistering heat streams in the mind's fog
Time is a sceptre dropped in thirst
The streets are still
And those who are working curse
Every nuance of imperfection.
But music, sweet music
Rolls out a carpet of ice
To dispel the summer
Day? What day?
Words creep with inner thunder
Across a sky of wooden beams.

When Jonah entered the whale
Perhaps it was like this in the deep –
A sway of ritual surrender
Which threatens reason
Like in Pleijel's Polonaise In A Major:

*"There is a music that can really drown us
if we don't lock it up behind bars."*

Well Agneta, the criminals are loose!

Family of Soil

Once you touch a hammer, beware:
A judge lies in its handle
And in the tune of the charcoal fork
Come rays of cloaked light
Books stand upon the shelves
And a bar stool tries to see above the bench
Where a fan moves hot air
Easels are gathered
And present in patience
News from another world
Compelling and unbelievable.
I have touched the hammer and tuned the fork
And in the distance I can hear
The baying of soundless dogs
Which circled the cathedral yard
In Saint Petersburg's streets.
Hunger doesn't have a name
Neither do beggars
Throat is a parched word
And dust is the secret
Which blankets in earthen gold
The family of soil
Made destitute in the anonymous world
Which brushes away stories
Without a second glance.

Dust

Upon the gold of the dust
Of the woman of soil
You will find God's kingdom
A blanket of earth shields her body
From the sun
Lowered her eyes pray through muslin
To vacancy and death
Promises which came from the
Tattered gift of birth
Let us lower our eyes
To the ground
Until we see with hidden vision
The field of her passion
Embracing the cold
Embracing the heat
And ignored by the cool dogs
Which sniff around her feet.
The wind has removed the invitation
There will be no repose
And no reflection
The dogs walk on stilts
Which endlessly seek the ground
Vertigo is the state
Marked by a flag of earth
Somewhere in space
Nowhere in time
Which died like a falling feather
From one of Attar's birds
A hand moves in her shroud
There is life there still
In the invitation removed by the wind

Which ripples in her reflection
Of our gaze
Which is her gaze;
Of Tarkovsky's black dog,
Nature's wandering beast
Who bays through this storm of dust.

Across the Salt Pan

The night is swollen with the cinders of day
And wax gleams like pliable bronze
Temptation has fled
Into the arms of music
Who left a violin in the hands
Of Finnish trolls
Via a drawing in Helsinki.
Time wanders from the artist's
Sleeping minstrel
With cupped hands of fresh water
Across the salt pan
Where have fallen those
Who didn't ask for anything
And those who asked for all
Predictably in mounds of salt
Humanity is growing.
Icilio awakened the pageant
In the minstrel's eyes
In ink
With a hand of forever
That music would arc across the salt pan
Proclaiming dreams of silver
And stirring life
In the parched mirage
Spreading through inconsolable heat
A cool wind of notes inspiring hidden limbs
To remember the dance
Which springs in the flowing river

Shadows on the Ground

So the wound up toy is ringing
In a cyclic awakening
Of programmed words
For the puppet which must jangle
To a tune marked out by agreed neurosis
If it weren't for amber consolation
The clock could go to hell
When ideas of us warmed
On a bloody patch of them
Where lay the head of another
Whose head is our own
Whose shadow is our shadow
And whose blood is our blood
Spreading upon the tight packed thought
Of the ground
Which doesn't invite
Which doesn't believe
Which resists all
In its soundless
Un-writable revolving of suns
Like the holy man rolling on the roads of India
But enlarged to fill the universe
Of the imperceptible blue.
The music of the ground
Is the essential music
If it weren't for that infernal toy
We would hear it
Growing in a pulse of geological anger
Against our material destitution.

The Painter

It is almost time for the burning to recede
And re-emerge in another shade
What tale blasted hand
Wrapped in skin and lifted by bone?
It is not for you to declare slaked thirst
No the fire whispers on
In an empty town
In a converted bank
On the shores of the rail line
Whose metallic eye
Catches a thousand miles of sun
There the painter works
Beyond care of state
Above commands of ambition
Upon heat which swells in a molten river of song
Friend of all
Lover of Time
Imp in the shadow
Gleaming with laughter
On roads of forever
In pace with the clouds
And the crumbling earth
Which look with a tender eye
Inside the soul of one
Refracting their atomic submersion
In a storm of red and bolts of magenta
Cadmium deep and yellow light
Skidding with the sun's new found physicality
In balance with a resounding
Intonality
Measured by the fever of a sceptre
Found somewhere in the bush

The Music

Hands baked
Through the city night
In a prayer of nocturnal busses
Which pulled out of blinking eyes –
That road never rests.
How sore the vein
Under the wounded earth
Which carries our world
In a hammock of concrete
Shovelled in the summer sun
By other hands which know work
Which form tough skin
And glistening muscle
Before an onset of cool amber
Mingles with the sweat.
The road looks up
At blackened figs
Their limbs wavering
In the carbon wind
Above tired prams
And students returning
From the university's stone hush.
Above this place awoke vision
Distant, ethereal, pulsing
In a parting of the sky
In a blaze of hidden music
Which dispelled a lonely haiku poem
Seeking to know autumn
A corner of rubber, lights, and screeching trucks
Accompanied an eternal hymn

Which was sensed in the brush
Of Paul Cezanne
In a country called France
Where we all want to go
But here it is
Above the heads of carbon touched figs:
The music

Tables of Wine

Tables of wine
Stood in an evening glade
Giving light resonance
In the stroke of O'Brien's hand
A spell of colours un-named
Stoked the gentle fire
Of a silent witness
Of Spirit's ethereal hand
Which picked up wine in a palette of song
And breathed in the Tuscan air
Floating upon a river which I know.

Justin, let me take your hand
As you sail passed -

But you are gone
And I must find my own raft.

Dear Patrick

Patrick, I remember every word and glance:
A Teacher of Olympian dreams
With blue feathers in your eyes
You transform skin
Into a miracle of light
Like that artist
Whom you love,
Georges De La Tour
The candle of France
Who spelled a light feathered silence
In your heart
Breathing into icons
Spirit's elemental gaze
With a hand trembling
With the hidden wand
Of a thousand years of art.
Ceilings have opened
In the mastery of your mind –
Call to their chains of mystery
Elope with their mistress of song
Which Cries with the trampled earth
And keep gazing, fearless Friend
Into that Petersburg night
Where the light of your fever wanders
With endless nostalgia
Along the bridges of the Neva
And in the wide parade
Of a thronging, destitute, and fire blinded humanity

Tunji and Fernando

The hand knows its craft
Like water
Supporting the air
The tappling of the tabla
Raises the immaterial
Material steps
Of the Dancer

Fernando strikes the floor
With staccato threats
Which hammer our hearts in silence
Imploding the heart with a measure
Of fierce reminders
In the tapping

Of a growing fury
Stillness conceals
And stops
When hands hover
And balance
The immaterial material becoming.

From the distance
In soft space
They grow and are growing
The hands of fury
Rising in a staccato wind
Of flashing pastel –

The curtain hides the light
And the wire hides a dancer

The Magic Cat is Singing

Tireless, unforgetting
The hand burns
Secretly
In a long sunlit night
Music, must I hold your cup forever?
Do you not sleep
Winged element?
Pastures are burning
In the crushing month of January
This is the country of salt pans
Where anonymous fires wander insatiably
Without surrender
A country without a name
And without a face
With shadows
Of haze
Colluding with silent geology
In a natural conspiracy.
Water drops
With slow dramatic intensity
The pasture's mouth is open
And steams in one momentous dense hour of rain -
Hidden in the castle
Cats are playing
With Balthus' ball of colour
Ania, the magic cat is singing
Would you like to hear ?
Yes? Then close your eyes.

II
Rings of Blue

Uncovered

Uncovered
You are beautiful
Sleeping in the morning sun.
Linsay's air is the dance of Pan,
A miracle of birds
Which flood the sky of our hearing,
With volleys of staccato lightning
From Tunji Beier's tips.
To look
With the temperature of a gaze
Into the
Dance -
His hooved splendour
Is Picasso's ardour,
Balancing the tragedy of the blinded bull
In hands which looked at him
With the wariness of a stranger,
And a friend,
Bitten in the cold hour.
Now I understand the wisdom of the Buddha
Energy is respiteless
And must be overcome,
To find the great expanse
Of ever floating eyes
In the breeze of vast openings,
Which in cool
Lift the air
In a shiver of soundless song.
Farīd ud-Dīn Attar, can you spare some wings?
Find your own
That is your joy and your challenge.

Gentle Blue

I am awake
I am asleep
Paper is a child
And wire is a song
Which rises
In voices from Giotto's choirs
Untraceable quavers
Upon the walls of distant Assisi.
How slow the river
How eternal
As Akhmatova's ageless muse
The walls of songs
Form invincible heiroglyphs
And shields of icons blazing with cool gold
My hands are empty
In the stillness of the night
Empty as the upturned palms
Of the Brothers
Standing at the ancient harvest
Behind wooden pews in darkness
One voice rises
The others follow
A gentle ring of blue
Forms around their sadness
Which looks towards the veil
Of a distant cinder
Hidden in the cloak
Of nowhere
Father
Voices ring around
In arcs of deepening blue

And another life
Ships feathers of silence to the mountain
You must climb
With light concealed in your hands
Up
Forever
With birds circling in the trees
Of a sacred life
Written in a message
Of floating notes from Giotto's walls

Offering

This journey is an untamed
Growth of blue neon rings
Touching the limbs of nowhere
Listen child of the dark
To this music hidden in my hands:
Every tower is a grace of astonished birds
Which resound in Attar's living kingdom
Gold has arisen from the desert's pan
As a shock of morning water
On a face glaring in the sun
A face touched by the heat
And cooled by the hands
Of a nameless brother
Who holds out a cup of painted silver
This gift is taken
From a table in the darkness
Drink its spaceless draught
And be refreshed in the night
Where burning hands
Cannot reach you.

Beads

Strings of beads
Are growing in my hands
Beads for Mario
Beads for the song
Which remembers the secret reds
And emeralds of Gauguin
His paintings awaken, claim, and rejoin
And sparkle through the fog
Reordering the verse in speechless skies
Of deafening vermillion
In bodies of golden hue
And a bird which flares
In a bright winged message from the cerulean shade
Passing its fruit into my hand
Into my chain
Of colour
Which wanders
Into the deep space
Of the growing castle
Gathering in my beads.

Rings of Blue

Rings of blue
Are gathering
Around the tower
In a hush of stone
Silent birds parade the grounds
In search of wisdom's element
A voice inflects
An eye gazes back
And insomnia wanders through the gates
The gates which are locked
Which have always been locked
For the soundless dogs
Which play in the dark
With the animal curiosity
Of Freedom
A nightmare of wonder
Is rolling through the world
Tired and profound
Fresh and lost
A table of silver
Stands in the clearing
Carved by Ricky Swallow
To hold the wine of O'Brien
In respite of endless journeys
Through rings of blue
Deep in humanity's ether

Surrender

The fire in the house
Is dwindling
Blackened coals are sleeping
And the walls shiver
With new sounds
Arriving
In a parade of slow and beautiful lights
The candles of Georges de La Tour
The glow of gold in the dim
Where Balthus' cat has played
Surrender has found
The ball of wool
Which fell from a lonely tower
And cascaded like a meteor
In the brilliance of an eye

Child

A child is carrying
The broken wing
Of our young century
Grafted to his oil stained shoulder
Somewhere where we can't see
In the dust of a bleached
And tattered memory
Knowing only hunger
And the thirst of the earth
For his limbs
Limbs which hide the earth
Limbs which grow in heaving fissures
Un named and potent
As stories from a black tree
Hidden in the desert

Icon

A stair of fire
Blooms from the icon
Under the tips of a hand
Shaded by the cool light
Of centuries
Awakened
In the pulse of furious prayers
Countless witnesses hooded in the dark
Who breathed cold air
In the songs of Salve Reginas
Dust walked
And suffered
Through a river of bodies
Like the mother of India, the Ganges
And the icon sailed through propulsion
Of it's inner heat
Like Mozart's violin
Which danced through wars
To find the hands
Of a surprised musician
Whose soul had been sleeping
In the skin of a dark drum
Which now pounds
Which now breathes
In the cool heat of the icon

Ascension

A book dwells inside
From which lines fly
Silently to waiting hands
Like a falconer
Standing just beyond memory
At humanity's piano
A deep pageant of song
Is kindled in dust
Which cloaks the sun
And settles
Upon shapes
Formed in clay
By the sculptor
Waiting and working:
The ovens of anonymous hands
Who have shaped death
In the face of birds
And who have walked
Passed earth and memory
Into the book
Waiting to be ascended
In a surprise of life

Faithless

Faithless hands are wandering
Across
And up the stairs
Of the icon's fire
Between surrender and incredulation
Hands bitten
By the cold dog
In the mythical square
Hands cooled and held
By the unknown Brother
With gestures of mysterious glyph
The hyphen sounded
A call to inordinate music
And a breathing space
For tired dust
Whose feet walk without repair
Without memory
And without the name
Which screamed at its birth
A child with feet of bronze
A broken wing upon his shoulder
Faithless and faithful
To the call in the deep shroud
Of the icon

For Ania

You who love Chagall
In his myth of blue spears
You who frame Poland's clouds
With inner rain
Your cat is walking upon roofs of silver
You can hear the dancing
In those Chagallian darks
Hear these odes
Falling
Through a hemisphere of blue
They talk with your eyes
Follow where your hands dream
And caress ten thousand miles
Of winter
You who shine in the cold
My hand is yours
A dream of lost light
Frozen in the shadow

Rinsed in Night

Rinsed in night
Your hands pale
Unadorned
Simple
Eyes lowered
With the planes
Of forgetting
Temperature lowered
Steady
Removing the heart from stones
Which lay naked
Simple
And alone

For Osip

"...and the centuries / Surround me with fire."
- Osip Mandelstam

A hand from a passing boat
Lifts shadow
Cold is sung
And lifted
Into the boat of night
Bars creep along the moon
Silver cigarettes
Flaring in a cool torch
You wandered among
Reflections
A shadow of the song you were
Passing
Fragments of heaven
To those who stood with you

Akhmatova's Eyes

Slowly in silent rings
The bridges build.
Odes are forming
For a witness
Held within the cold lines
Of Russia's
Freezing square.
A memory of bread
Dropped crumbs
Into her eyes
Akhmatova's eyes
Which bled

Anna's Song

For Anna Akhmatova (1889 - 1966)

You carried the child Anna
The broken child of Russia
In your arms
In steps of
Snow
Which froze
In bitten tears
And gathered
In the black suns
Of your eyes
Where
In eternal sleep
God bathed and imagined
An immaculate dawn -
A frost of circles
In a flight of pillows
Soft
In the pale midnight
Of Anna's song

Shadows

Temperature
Keeps to itself
The soft ringing
Of secrets
Held in its hands
So take mine
In cups of wandering blue
Across the desert
Across love
Where the beating heart
Of Music
Lies upon the ground
Hold the heart in soft burning shadows
And whisper
To your beloved
In the night

Migration

For Icilio Martich-Severi (1920-1999)

The ground is endless
A fence lies desecrated
In the silence
Of the hills
Found far from the home
Of wandering birds
Arcing
In the prisons
Of Giovanni Piranesi
Who held space
In a needle upon a plate
For the table of Icilio Severi
To rewrite in ink
The lines of migration
Upon his bench
In stillness.
A dance rehearsal was held
Which in gentle arcs
Reawakened the birds
Of human courtship
In planes of distant shade
Awakening walked
Through rooms
Held in silence
With a conference far away
Mingling with piano notes
The imaginings
Of hands hidden and re revealed
In a human score
Of beaks
Glinting and alive

Donkey

Stars shone
In mist
Night's hands curled out
To lift
The deep air
Where gravity
Was held
In a silhouette of space
In the arms
Of distant memories
Which lay on the floor
On a mat
In the eye
Of a strange and mysterious world
Heat sung in the day
With the flute of thistles
Which gave up memory
In exchange
For light
A good bargain
In the geological store
On the top of a mountain
I rode a donkey
As simple
And straightforward
As that

Bach

There is no end to the blue
Like an unending Torah scroll
It unravels
In the cool of the night
Where hands played
The piano
In search of keys
Which found the fingers
Of Bach
Holy elemental Bach
God of tight packed thunder
Who stepped in perfect space
Upon the ringing of the spirit
Dogs howl
In the country side of grace
For the beauty
Of the soundless moon

Patrick's Hand

For Patrick Bernard

I am astonished
Beyond all imagining
The spatial light
Of god
Sings from the sepulcher
From within columns
Of Patrick's hand
Held in wondrous unity
With the waves
Of the mysterious source
Growing in cool fire
Upon the altar
And within eyes
Which grow wide
With an ethereal depth
In a space
Which knows the suns

Invitation

Upon the fields of Tarrawarra Abbey, Yarra Glen, Victoria.

An invitation
Was spoken
In the dark.
With invisible eyes he gazed
With a light
Which left the air
Transparent in every season.
Shining eyes
Gleamed in the chapel
Without veil, without audience,
With only the damp earth as witness -
That and an iron bell
Which intoned
The message to fields of prayer.
Swaying golden under stars,
Pierced by the dreams of bulls
And the clinking of gates
In gentle winds,
An audience hovered -
In the circle of endless suns,
In the daylight of great arrangements
Which opened between us
And waved in ceaseless splendour
Above the fields

Standing

Blue shadows
Advanced across the field
Where we stood
In an hour
Stolen
By the lake
Which rippled in ageless surprise
At the sight of the sky.
We held hands
Freed from others'
And smiled in surrender
Within the gentle peace
Of Arcadia

Pastoral

Temperature dwelt
Hidden in belts of grass
With the snake of day
Which fired the road
With glinting
Quartz
Taken from mute rock
Dogs bayed with senseless ardour
At footsteps
Which knew
And which didn't know
The path
Away from the castle
Hidden in the sudden rain

Cheek

I have lost Time
Where did he go?
The bastard owes me some money!

Dreams

The relief of midnight
Is temporary
So do not
Get hung up on shadow
Fires will come again
And blast
The cool air
With cinder
But not now
The universe is poised in sleep
Children are tucked into the dark
And mothers' faces glow behind soft lamps
Ready

Still and Washed

Still and washed
Hiding behind the rock
Dreaming sunlight into limbs
And forgetting the ode
Which never came
And flashed into disappearance

The Path

For James Clayden & Lawrence Gundabuka

It grows
The ring is tireless
It gathers
Into hoops of night
In Gundabuka's dance
Which awakened Giacometti
From Clayden's deep compression
A burial ground of space
Reconstructing thoughts
And building secret symphonies
From the ground
On concrete
In flourescent light
With cold un-arguing ambivalence
Restated it was restated
And the aim in Hamlet* doesn't exist
For there is no aim in the spiral
Which grows, which arcs
Which gathers and departs
Along beds of neon and soundless rivers
A music of unalterable quavers
Unraveling from the chest
Of spirit's flaming hand
And dumping in the dark
The bodies of deceased language
Like gangsters colluding in a secret coven
Which flashed in the white ring
And knew
With sudden absolute knowing
The path

Harvest of Suns

The surprise of the sun
With its cloak of darkness
Furrowed
By the seamstress of space
With a needle wide and cold
The harvest of suns
In slow blaze
Stoked the fire of the icons
Whose cases of gold
Wavered
And spoke
Of the spiritual sister of the physical sun
A bilingual birth
Uniting
The stars' seamless majesty
With the earth

The Pieces Fall

Breathing in the silence
Of an endless night
The cats are playing
With Balthus' ball again
With an occasional screech of displeasure
A silent game
Held in the square
Where the pieces float
From space to space
By design
Of the secret measure
Of the wool
In the tower
Cascading to where the pieces fall
In the mystery of an unknown jury

Arrangement

I am in the grip
Of an impossible space
Which closes its eyes
In order to open them
There is no sleep
For the Brother of Time
Whose faithless prayers
Mingle in the dark
With Rembrandt's
River
Balthus' cats, and Borges' sparkling edifices
Rain has come will come
It is the time of endless rain
Which grows and will grow and has always grown
On the field
On the mountain of Kafka's sorrow
And the magic of Thomas Mann
The mysterious mountain of infinite
Arrangement
Growing in the dark in the light
Beyond the tap
Of earth
In a wild birth of ceaseless
Unceasing
In the silent exquisite turning
Of the
Blazing tap of Now

Promise

The towers face the earth
There is no other face
And the embrace of solitude
Falls
In the quiet hour
Fire is a harmless blanket of dust
Which shears the invisible
With speechless knowing
Inviting the speech
Of the animal
Playing in the square
The cinder remains a particle of promise
To be fed to the dogs
In the coming night

Blue Fire

Icons in the shadow
Blaze in somnolent ardour
Gold in the grass
Is speaking a mass of silver
Grazed
And un quenched
The blue fire rages
A hymn of unending spirit
A quail of bright feathered silences
Which moves and grows
With a hidden fist
Gazing in a line
Into
Eternal eyes

Ageless Songs

Ageless songs are
Lining the fire of space
Deathless and strong
As a shield of icons
Burning in the blue night
Heralds are awakening in the stones
And a speech filled hand
Tumbles in stories of gold
A shower of hidden rain
Behind the eyes
Floating breathless
In an ascending
Howl of Freedom

The Blue Universe

There is a power in my eyes
Sleepless, pure
Which rings
In spears of shadow
The Blue Universe
Has awoken
And streams with cool fire
Upon the glass
In deep winter
Rasping
With a furious pageant
Of unending suns
Revolving in magical splendour
Around a ring of unimaginable blue

The Endless Suns

A golden dancer
Fell into the song
Never will space be the same
As when it faced
The Endless Suns
Which gathered into storms of light
And arced
With glowing music
Which was cindered
Pure
And governless

Cold

Cold
White new pages
Are marching
In a parade of sleepless nights
Lighting fires
Cool
Strong
With hands
Burning
With eyes
Burning
Cindered
Powerless

Kiefer's Song

Anselm Kiefer forged
A wing
A child
Made of lead
And truth
Mixed with the pitch
Of Wolund
Bronzed, leaded
Disabled in a silent field
Choked
With descent
And stillness

Reflections

Chased by dogs
In the dark
I have spelled
My name backwards
In Time's mirror
Which allows no reflections
Save one eno evaS

Caress

My vision is intense
Sometimes frightening
But also as soft
As pale blue lightning
Which touches your lids
In an ultimate caress
Of sorrow
And wonder

The Black Dog

Rings of silent eyes are watching
In a company of despair
Birds are building bridges
In the quiet blue
A verse of sorrow
And cerulean cinder
Is marching in the shade
Watched by a black dog
Crossing the unknown

Where is the Hammock?

I'm lost
I'm held
The beautiful cindered mind is growing
A cavern bright airy
Dark mysterious
Giotto's walls in Rembrandt's nights
Come, where is the hammock?
I grow sleepy
Tales are for night time
To hell with them

Tale of the Hammock

It broke

Fists of Now

Cameras are rolling on the horizon
Eyes are burning in soft shadow
The cats are playing in Balthus' tower -
This is a hymn that I know.
Born in looping arcs of playful fire
Dreaming in the cerulean deep
Alive with children
Playing in the sand
With buckets full of gold,
Shipped from a hidden desert
By spades that know digging.
Thank you Seamus Heaney
For your furrowed earth,
For the wing of your shade
Which punches the air
In blinding staccato beats,
Talking into the wilderness of loss, love, politics,
Of We, of Then, in Fists of Now
In pointed rhythms of bright becoming.
Objects have lost their place in my vocabulary,
A fan whirs in impotent reproach;
It stirs the studio air,
Stale and silent
But for a lash of vowels
Cascading through the day -
A course of meteors
Concealed in the blue

III

Blinded Bulls

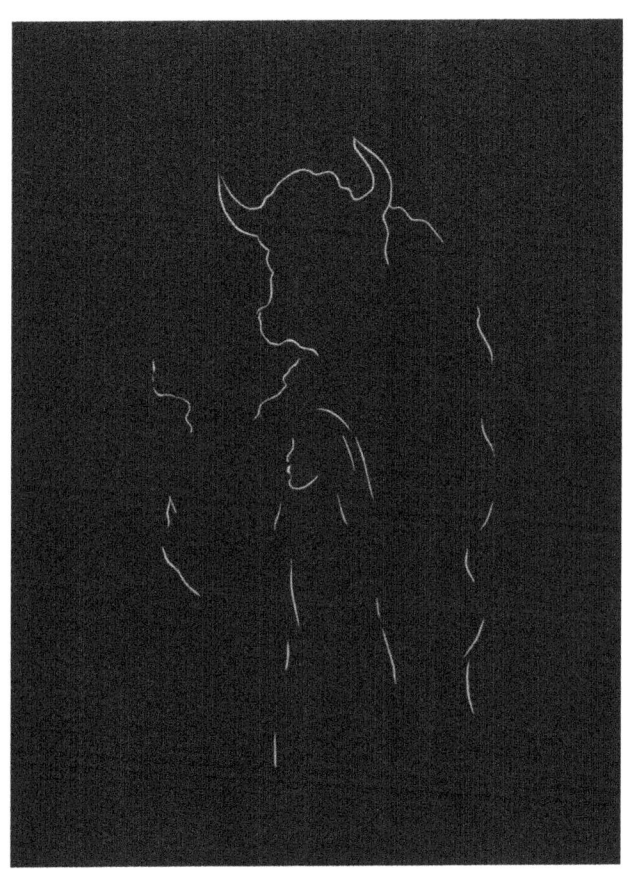

The Tree of Alchemy

Charcoal which burns in wings of gold
Is enflaming the limbs of the black tree
Hidden in balance with the blue rose
Whose petals cinder in the shade
Magnificent alchemy reveals its flutes
In tight packed thunder
Which revels in the steps of invisible Bach
Calamity is the word which frightens the wind
Which razes the earth
Until its rocky beds quiver in stillness
And force
A mighty tide to grow from within the bowels of the
Ocean
Tabling the song of forever
In a high arc -
Floating somewhere at sea for an infinite age
Of coconut water
And dying friends
A miracle of time has harnessed
A wing of life
To
Wordlessness
To gone
To the enquiry of geological anger
Snapping in ferocious abandon the branches
Of the tree
Hidden in darkness
Smouldering in gold lit charcoal
Whose trunk is the shaft
Immeasurable
And burnt

A Rain of Blood

If the world ran out of fire
I would hold it in my pen
Like Breughel's Mad Griet
Scared in the Flemish haze
Sword glinting in the spider's harp
A compression of sounds
Floating through organic hell
Whose eyebrows seat incalculable birds
And into whose mouth
Float the debris
Of infernal humanity's wounds
Arms floating by
The blackened limbs of Palestine
And her mirror of fury: Israel
Where God was born in nights of slaughter
Which continued
In the hunt for calvary
And a lamb
Born for pain
In secret wisdom
Of an artist hellbent on devastation
In the advent of the possibility
That it will begin again
In incredible forgetting
A rain of blood
Is shielding humanity
From life

Blinded Bulls

Terrifying riches shake the dark tower
The blinded bull has walked into the square
Led by Love
Who with discordant steps
Frees the pageant of the unknown
These are no longer rings but bulls
Tragedy's steps
In the beat of a child
And hands of silent fury
Which recall Tunji Beier's tips
The embers have quickened
A dance lies on the air
They are back, the stones
Which rested in the blue
Respite has had its fill
Now to war!

The Dogs of Midnight

My hand remembers the lines in the air
Gyrating forms in the blackened square
Glinting their teeth in the ferocious sun
The dogs of midnight have begun

Thunder

Raging bulls of the earth
Backs decked with fire
Walking on tectonic plates
With feet of cinder
Roaming with restless breath
Under the creeping planet
Eyes hidden dark blind
In mines of sulphur
Which gathers in a broad ring
Around the town of gold
Break dance into your trembling spirit
With staccato strikes
Remember Fernando and the blistering tabla
Rising and falling growing and bracing
Into a wondrous war
Of thunderous becoming

Minotaur

My face is burning
Years are sailing by in minutes
Have I spoken
Of He
Holding spears of night
In the corridors of time?
No?
Then hear this:
Hard headed darkness
Dwelt in shades
Bitten
With rolling songs
Of lustrous timbre
They came
In grades so deep
The river shivered
A giant trembling
With sorrow
He wandered
He was lost
A Minotaur
Roaming blind
Amongst the stars

Nocturne

It is time for sleep
Thunder must wait
For the glinting eye of sadness
To return with spears of shadow
When gold will gaze into gloom
And spread its rivered treasure
Sleep pen
Sleep

Insomniacs of Nature

In a pageant of burnt shadows
The bulls returned
Rumbling in the sleeping earth
Discovering sounds of thunder
Hidden in a pen of stabbing silver
Sleepless they roamed
Insomniacs of nature
Blackened, bold,
Staked and dreamt
Blazing with wounds
Into inconsolable Goya's oils
Where his thundering
Collossus stepped
And with quiet knocks in the dead of night
Spread terror throughout Spain
Which fell in carbon ash
In odes of deepening fury
Onto pastures
Where bulls drank blood
And celebrated in the night
With songs coarse and dark
The victories of cold and blinded Lethe

Pale Thunder

Pale Thunder came
In the beating wings of birds
A message from Dante's crypt
Of blood and sacrifice
Burning hands dipped into glistening pools
Where fell in a terrible stench
The bodies of humanity
Macbeth incarnadine
And the witches at the well
Stepped out of dreams
And into Breughel's Hell
Flaming in wars untold
Where crept Lethe in fields of dark
Through the shadows of Bush's hands
And suffocating in songs of fear
The creatures of the earth

On Picasso

Thunder is coming
Are you ready?
Growing in the shade
A sleeping Minotaur
The breath of Picasso's hands
Which clapped
To a soundless toreador
Circling the beast
Which with each clap then did twitch
And flick its dreaming tail
Picasso, who with hands of bronze
Rose from this quiet ground
A father and a son of death
Dreamt of cool
In myth's slim waist
And found a charging bull!

Gold Rain

Gold rain has come
Into frightened morning
Bulls of myth in streaming cold
The lights of distant Greece
Burning in the shade
Of southern timbre
Hands of speech
Rising from the ground
To ageless sounds
Bitten struck
And clapping
A dance of hidden pulse
Magic strong and bright
Caresses the yearning face
Of beauty's hidden night
Clap on hands Rise
On sounds
Of birth
And bless the wind
In its creeping song
On tables of morning light
Please sit down
Be my guest
And shower me with smiles

Land Mines

Land mines lay hidden
In the heart of the child
With the broken wing
His fingernails are shrapnel
Gathered from the blast
Which quakes distant Israel
And her fighting sister Palestine
Those sisters, orphaned
By other sisters
Who fought in rings of gathering sorrow
Around the blackened tree
Marking attempts to sever
Its great and mighty shaft
An inversion of the genders
From Poussin's Grecian intervention
Where women fell and rose
In wails of remonstration
O Maltese hand of undying blood
Take this shroud
And wash those forsaken feet
Stained
In the blood of mines
Which deface the child
With every shrapnelled
Step

Oppenheimer's Score

Clapping thunder rose
In the speech of Bach
Whilst Beethoven slept and dreamt
In furious unending
The soul of drunk Shostakovic
Staggered in the rain
Whilst the chimes of Chopin
Tinkled at the door
Preparing the coming feast
For Oppenheimer's score
Of blinding fury
Blasting the timbre
Of a sadist century

Days Eternal

I'm on the way
It doesn't matter where
Into fury's deep midnight
Where the music is loud and long
A clashing of cymbals
Amidst a terrible feast
Of humanity's despair
Of wings singed in a golden haze
In Wolund Kiefer's song
Infamous bulls are drinking
Without halt
In a blaze of thirst unquenched
In those rings of blue
Up tempo
Speed fire
Rain into the dark
With your whips
Of frightening teeth
The birth is dangerous
The days eternal
Let them come
And weep upon my shoulder

Warning

The book is an experience
Of meteoric flares
Joining hands of passion
In gesticulating arcs
Which fired Jackson Pollock's limbs
In dances frayed and dangerous
As loose wires in the rain
Be careful hands of passion
Take heed of his warning
Row deep and soundless
With a head of solid bronze
And eyes which vanish
In splendours undefined
By the sniffing of hounds
Around the dead

Monstrous Wire

It's raining
A child is born
A hidden light
Is glowing in my hands
Distant thunder trundles
With the trolleys down below
The screeching Banshee's pitch
Has hit a trembling line
Of nerves
Throughout the tower
Dogs in the mythic square
Pace with new found life
And Balthus' rolling ball
Of wool has changed into monstrous wire
Flaying
In a wild wind
Of hidden suicide

Untouched

Dogs in space
Eat the dark
Alsations of supine measure
The game is afoot
It is friendly fire
A round of playful spars
Which hold the air
In a familial embrace
Stepping backwards without care
A family of struggles which flew
In Rubens'
Furia del pennello
The canines, in soundless rings
Fight for all of nature
Which breathes at last
In fields untouched
By humans

Songs Unfathomable

Today is rounded with swallows of fire
Arcing from Mandelstam's verse
And Dante's heat
A cinder of creatures arriving
On the table
Of unfathomable songs
Fly swallows, brave friends
Into the unflinching truth
A masquerade of lies from Death
Who streams
In ever increasing winds
Across the face of earth

Lorca's Guitar

A pause of wounded bulls
Lined up in the night
Swaying in the shadow
Hiding in the length
Of wooden imagining
Which framed the distant meadows
Under weeping stars.
Lorca, your guitar,
I found it by the road.
Here -
But you are gone.
Must I play?

Shield

Shales of human forgetting
Have arrived on the window pain
Deep rain is floating
Through my heart
Mother, brother
Tales combined
To lift a shining shield
From my astonished hands

Blinded Lethe

I am breathless with discovery
And wounded by the glare
Of the gored and shrapnelled child
Bronze fists of anger immeasurable
A wing of leaden death
You make me transparent
With your pain
Now I understand Christ
Whose limbs flared and shone
Like mirrors
Like glass
Which shattered and fell
In a rain of transcending passion
Upon the fields
Of blinded Lethe
Who, feeling glass soft as snow
Looked up in astonishment
At the son of man

Ships

Wings of shadow move
At a mysterious bequest
A cloak has fallen to the floor
Naked
Exposed
Feel the pain
In my voice
A voice of searing spears
Thrown at the raging bulls
In one momentous hour of rain –
With hands of bronze
Discovery holds out its cup
For the journey
Of distant
Ships
Chained
On humanity's horizon

Gone

The wounded bulls
Stand glaring
On
Paths forsaken
By lonely light
In the rain
Hidden beyond memory
Gores flashing
Stumbling
Pounding
Pleading for respite
From spears endlessly thrown
Where is the Minotaur?
His song of deep midnight?
Lost
Stumbling
Gone

Albatross

The ships of furious memory
Are shadowing the song
With horns blaring
And search lights beaming
For the child of Lethe's ghost
On the wing of Sammuel's ode
The albatross is here
With wings which span
Across the sky of fearless imagining
Nature's gift
To those whose hands are burning
With interminable shadows.
Fly Tragedy
You are beautiful and light
My song is for you

Gilding

Horizon's cup sits
On a table pale and gold
Take a sip of distant
Songs
Refresh your eyes
Ignite your hands
Here take mine
And gild

Pale Gold

The furious measure of an eye
Dipped in wax
And cast in bronze
Is scaling the surrendered trophe
Of a fishing ladder.
Chagall would understand
The reason for blazing fish
Which flew in Balthus' mind
Before it searched for limbs
Pale and gold,
Breathing in the dawn
Falcons of enchanted youth,
Perched on light
Between eternal paintings rim.
Do not turn off the light
The bulls stagger still

Wealth

A rain of wealth
Is startling my eyes
Which squint without respite
Thank you piano keys
For this new found thunder
Which breaks
Which sears
Bending time into crimson tears
Friends hold me
I am swaying
The wind is howling
And I cannot block it out

Growth

The furies of midnight grow
Into something
Held
Something remembered
Into pain
Into limbs
And hidden masses
Into rites of Easter
Which raise with blood stained arms
Signs of a transcendent martyr
Gold washed in blood
A heretic's shroud
Which now covers war
In limp light
A tragedy of messages lost
The failure of the Vatican
Come now, take this hand
And grow

Vision

Elemental fury is blurring my vision
If I go blind
The colours of pale gold
Will still resound in my hands
And fly with Samuels's albatross
Through grief
Stricken
Pure as an unrelenting ode of vision
Rising into the astonished sky
Forming bonds which break
But travelling still
With Andrei's tattered skins
Over the rivers of lost thoughts
And children
Who look up in wonder

Promises

For Harry

Promises broken in your eyes
O gentle giant of pastel
You flew airplanes on the ground
In enormous caverns
Which released the gifts of air
Into distant war
You gaze into light
Finding colour
With soft cindered shadows
Grazing from your hand
The promise remains
And will not break
It will hold
Into eternity

In the Libraries of Night

In the libraries of night
I sing
Notes from forgotten choirs
Bulls are led by pale gold hands
Into peaceful pasture
Where rings and shadows lay
In soft blue cinder
The Minotaur is singing
Deep, soft, and bold
A lullaby for burning hands
And mirrors
Which reflect in meteoric bolts
The distant hymns of war
Feeding Goya's trembling hands
As a bull charges out of gold
And back into the light

Lethe's Shadow

Peaceful drums are ringing
In the child's bloody ears
Is this respite or pause?
Does gold beckon or delay
The hands of fury
Pounding through the mist?
Lethe's shadow dims
The bulls are gone

Tips of Fire

Tips of fire
Are singing through the grass
Tunji Beier's hands
Are pounding through the rock
Restless songs are rising
Aching through the earth
The hands of fury rip and pound and move
Trembling with reminders
Of lost children
Wandering with the Minotaur
On stairs
Of stars

Tales of the Mirror

Prologue

Soft burning shadows
Are forming in my hands
Cindered rings
And a blackened tree
From which hung a voice
Lost and gone
O sacred Minotaur
Song of deep midnight
Take care of this wandering child
Who leads you
On your path
She is wounded –
Scared
She needs healing –
Beyond

I

Pages curl in the rain
As the Minotaur is singing
But it is not enough
Deeper in the world
Stands a mirror
Silent
Alone
Frightened

II

In whispers
The mirror sings
That it may shine
And recall light

III

In a basement
She sings
With bitten shadows

IV

A bull is standing
With eyes of gold
In the mirror

V

Boom Boom
A feather in the deep
An age of relentless darks
Rolling in human rings
And mirrors
Which burn

VI

    Shadows

             Walk

                      Into

              Me

      Let

              Them   be

                  In   Me

                      In

                  Lost

                        Mirrors

    Lost

                  In

                    Me

                In

         Mirrors

VII

Dear Reader: this ode is to be read twice from "With" and ending on the second cycle with "hands". Read the first four lines, then clockwise from "The Deep…"

Glinting	With a voice of	
silver	Glinting silver	The
Of	And shadows	Deep
Mirrors	Replacing hands	Song
Lost		Lost
Of		Its
Pageants		Way
In		Lost
Mirrors		In

VIII

Araiadne's light
Found Balthus' ball
In dark
To trace our steps
Out of
Burning mirrors

IX

Take his hand child
Lead him out
The way is dark
You will need
Eyes
Of
Burning cool
And a friend in the shadow

X

The cats are playing
With Mystery's wool
Which cascaded from the tower
Leading Ariadnes light of cool
And cindered power

XI

From shadow a reflection grew
A mountain from Attar's verse
A wound of nature
Billy Goat Hill
Damage on the breeze
And the eyes of the Minotaur
In the sockets of the child

XII

Labyrinths of passion transparent
Mirrors of eyes in the day
Look with surrender
Sky O so blue
Traces of gold in your hand

Epilogue

Music reawakened in a hymn
Of love's first kiss
Of gentle eyes
Streaming in
Blue wind
With cool and furious power
Hands which locked with gentle keys
As Lethe's hounds
Wandered out of time

Poor Lethe

Poor Lethe
Blinded in the cold
Destroyed by war
Before
Your eyes were sold

NOTES ON THE POEMS
I. Burning Stones

Doubt (p.14)
"Kurasawa's Demons" refers to characters in Akira Kurasawa's film 'The Dreams of Kurasawa. "Pygmallion's gaze" refers to the Greek myth of Pygmallion who prayed for his sculpture to be brought to life.

Haze (p.16)
References are made to Francisco de Goya's painting 'The Colossus' (1808-1812), Picasso's iconic composition 'Guernica' (1937) and 'The Feast of Venus' by Peter Paul Rubens (1636). Whilst 'The Colossus' and 'Guernica' both depict the horrors off war, 'The Feast of Venus' is a frenzy of Dionysian pleasure and indulgence. According to tradition, however, it was the pleasure of Herod's daughter Salome, to be delivered the head of John the Baptist. "the unknown child / The Invisible Friend hidden in the cloak of war" is the first mention in 'Insomnia's Gates' of the archetypal figure of the 'Wounded Child'. *See also Untouched (p.129) and 'Wounded Child' under Recurring Motifs and Symbols.*

Impotence (p.24)
Reference is made to the Russian poet Anna Akhmatova (1889-1966), whose poetry stands as a witness and testament to the endurance and struggle of the Russian people under Stalinism. See also *Chambers of Autumn Fire* (p.49), *Akhmatova's Eyes* (p.81), *Anna's Song* (p.82).

Milosz's Sail (p.28)
The poem refers to the great Lithuanian/Polish poet Czeslaw Milosz (1911-2004), whose poetry (in translation) has acted as a catalyst for the author. See also *Chambers of Autumn Fire* (p.49).

Rembrandt's Eyes (p.32)
"Mandelstam's gold" refers to the poetry of the Russian poet Osip Mandelstam, known to the author through the translations of Bernard Meares. See also: *Chambers of Autumn Fire* (p.49), *For Osip* (p.80), *Songs Unfathomable* (p.130). Further references to Rembrandt: *Arrangement* (p.97), *Where is the Hammock?* (p.108).

The Master (p.41)
The poem recalls the studio of Italo-Australian artist Icilio Martich-Severi, where the author resided for several months following the artist's death in 1999. The studio was divided by several large flat-colour compositions suspended in fibre glass ("castles of colour"). In one corner two sculptures, "Adam" and "Eve" stood watch. The "case of gold" refers to icons the author was painting in Martich-Severi's studio. See also: *Across the Salt Pan* (p. 56) and *Migration* (p. 84).

Remonstration (p.48)
"Bacon's pinks and reds" refers to the signature colours used by the Irish/English painter Francis Bacon.

Chambers of Autumn Fire (p.49)
References are made here to the following poets: Anna Akhmatova and Osip Mandelstam (Russian), Czeslaw Milosz (Lithuanian/Polish), Paul Celan (Romanian/French), Farīd ud-Dīn Attar and Rumi (13th century Persian). Reference is also made to the poet-song writer Leonard Cohen (Canadian) and the 18th century composer Antonio Vivaldi (Italian), as well as the 20th century painter Balthus (Balthasar Klossowski de Rola) (French/Polish). "The Sphinx of Moonbi" refers to a large granite boulder which lies at the foothills of the Moonbi Ranges in northern N.S.W. Australia. In the eye of the author the lichen on the boulder formed the image of a sphinx.

Quavers (p.51)
"Croque Monsieur" refers here to an Australian French-Gypsy ensemble.

Criminal Music (p.52)
The quotation is taken from: 'Poems by Agneta Pleijel: Eyes From A Dream' . Translated by Anne Born for Forest Books 1991. *Polonaise In A Major: 3* (page 5 lines 11-12).

Dust (p.54)
"...a falling feather from one of Attar's birds" refers to the birds who search for their king (God) in 'The Conference of the Birds", a spiritual classic by the 13th century Persian Sufi poet Farīd ud-Dīn Attar. See also: *Chambers of Autumn Fire* (p.49), *Uncovered* (p.67), *Offering* (p.70), *Tales of the Mirror XI* (p.152). "Tarkovsky's black dog" refers to the dog in Andrei Tarkovsky's film 'Stalker'. In the film the dog is a free agent and seemingly immune to the dangers of 'the zone'. *See also 'Dogs', 'Birds' and 'Farīd ud-Dīn Attar' under Recurring Motifs and Symbols.*

Across the Salt Pan (p.56)
The poem initially refers to an etching by the Finnish artist Hugo Simberg, titled 'Swan Song', mistakenly remembered here as a drawing. In the image three small naked devils (remembered here as trolls), holding instruments, stand next to the prostrate figure of a musician, his mandolin (remembered here as a violin) discarded beside him. "Icilio" refers to the artist Icilio Martich-Severi, whose studio the author briefly resided in following the artist's death in 1999. See also: *The Master* (p. 41) and *Migration* (p. 84).

Tables of Wine (p. 61)
The poem makes reference to the Australian painter Justin O'Brien (1917-1996) who worked in Tuscany for the latter part of his life. O'Brien's work is a touchstone for the author, who is also (and mainly) a visual artist. See also: *Rings of Blue* (p. 72).

Dear Patrick (p.62)
Georges de La Tour was a 17th century French Baroque painter, a favourite of the author's painting mentor at university, Patrick Bernard, whom the poem is addressed to. See also: *Patrick's Hand* (p. 87).

Tunji and Fernando (p.63)
The poem recalls a performance by Tunji Beier, an outstanding world percussionist, and Fernando, a Flamenco dancer. Tunji Beier's music takes on an almost archetypal character role in *Rings of Blue* and *Blinded Bulls*, the two collections which follow *Burning Stones*. See also: *Song of the Tavil* (p. 23), *Uncovered* (p.67), *Blinded Bulls* (p.115), *Thunder* (p.117), *Tips of Fire* (p.145) and *'Tunji Beier's Tips'* under Recurring Motifs and Symbols.

The Magic Cat is Singing (p.64)
"Balthus' ball of colour" invokes the work of the French/Polish painter Balthus, who often depicted cats within his compositions. The popular image of a cat playing with a ball of wool is here conflated with the colours of the paint box. *See also 'Balthus' ball of colour' under Recurring Motifs and Symbols.*

II. Rings of Blue

Uncovered (p.67)
The poem conflates two etchings by Picasso ('Pan' and 'Minotauromachy') with the music of Australian collaboraters Linsay Pollock and Tunji Beier. The "blinded bull" is a reference to Picasso's blind minotaur in his etching 'Minotauromachy', a prophetic glimpse of the cycle which follows 'Rings of Blue'. "Farīd ud-Dīn Attar, can you spare some wings?" references the Persian poet's spiritual classic, 'The Conference of the Birds'. *See also 'Blinded Bulls', 'Farīd ud-Dīn Attar' and 'Tunji Beier's Tips' under Recurring Motifs and Symbols.*

Gentle Blue (p.68)
"Giotto's choirs" is a synaesthesic expression of painted colour as sound, imagining Giotto's fresco cycle in the Bascillica of St Francis, Asissi, as voices from a choir.

Rings Of Blue (p.72)
The lines, "A table of silver / Stands in the clearing / Carved by Ricky Swallow", refers to a sculpture by the Australian artist Ricky Swallow, called 'Killing Time'. The sculpture is of a seafood banquet, carved entirely out of wood. In the poem Swallow's table holds "the wine of O'Brien", referring to the painter Justin O'Brien, where the 'wine' perhaps represents colour or spirit or art itself. See also *Tables of Wine* (p.61).

Surrender (p.73)
Georges de La Tour: French painter (1593-1652), whose work is suffused with soft candle light. See also: *Dear Patrick* (p.62). "Balthus' cat" refers to the cat in the paintings of Balthus (French/Polish), representing, perhaps, the playful mystery of art. *See 'Balthus' under Recurring Motifs and Symbols.*

For Osip (p.80)
In memory of Osip Mandelstam (1891 - 1938), the most cerebral voice of 20th century Russian poetry. In 1938 he was arrested and deported to the Soviet Far East for his artistic criticism of Stalin. He died anonymously in a transit camp, somewhere near Vladivostok. His 'Verses On The Unknown Soldier', written in 1937, concludes: "...and the centuries / Surround me with fire." (Ref: Mandelstam Poems; trans. Bernard Meares; Persea Books).

Akhmatova's Eyes (p.81)
For Anna Akhmatova (1889 - 1966). Reference to Akhmatova's poem 'Requiem', where the poet describes waiting in line, mid-winter, to see her imprisoned son.

Migration (p.84)
For Icilio Martich-Severi (1920-1999), a Fiumani- Australian modernist master who's work, to the author's mind, recalls the graphic genius of Giovanni Battista Piranesi (1720-1778). Martich-Severi migrated to Australia in 1950 from the formerly free state of Fiume, annexed in turn by Italy and Croatia. See also: *Across the Salt Pan* (p. 56), *The Master* (p.41).

The Path (p.94)
For James Clayden (Australian painter, sculptor, and filmmaker) and for Lawrence Gundabuka (Australian sculptor), whose works, to the author's mind, stand on either side of Alberto Giacometti's (Swiss sculptor and painter; 1901 - 1966).*Hamlet refers to James Clayden's 2004 film 'Hamlet X' which is structured upon the principle of scenic repetition.

Arrangement (p.97)
References are made here to the painters Rembrandt and Balthus, the Argentian poet Jorge Luis Borges, and two novelists, Franz Kafka and Thomas Mann. They are invoked almost as a literal landscape ("river", "cats", "edifices", "mountain"), with an allusion made to Thomas Mann's novel 'The Magic Mountain' (1924). *See also 'Balthus' under Recurring Motifs and Symbols.*

Kiefer's Song (p.104)
A reference to Anselm Kiefer's (post-war German artist) monumental 'Wolund's Song (with wing)', created in 1982. The title of this painting refers to a legend which is found in the Edda, a collection of Scandinavian myths. Kiefer fuses the narrative of Wolund, who fashions wings from lead in order to escape captivity, with the meta-narrative of the second world war, creating a work of tragic, alchemical stillness. The poem enlists Kiefer as an imagined co-creator of the 'wounded child' figure, who first appears in *Child* (p.74). *See also 'Wounded Child' under Recurring Motifs and Symbols.*

Fists of Now (p.110)
The poem invokes the by-now familiar image of Balthus' cats (see 'Balthus' cats' under Recurring Motifs and Symbols). The heart of the poem alludes to a famous poem by the great Irish poet Seamus Heaney, called *Digging*.

III. Blinded Bulls

The Tree of Alchemy (p.113)
The subject here is the Indian Ocean earthquake and tsunami of 2004 which killed over 200,000 people.

A Rain of Blood (p.114)
"Breughel's mad Griet" refers to Pieter Breughel's painting 'Dulle Griet' (translated as 'Mad Meg'). Dulle Griet, a figure from Flemish folklore, is depicted by Breughel with sword, breastplate, treasure and food, running, sword outstretched, through a scene of devilment and chaos. Ironically she appears to be the most sane figure in the image. The poem compresses this image with both the conflict between Palestine and Israel, and the 'Massacre of the innocents', following the birth of Christ.

Blinded Bulls (p.115)
See *'Blinded Bulls'*, *'Tunji Beier's tips'* and *'Wounded child'* under *Recurring Motifs and Symbols*.

Insomniacs of Nature (p.120)
Reference is made here to 'The Collosus', a painting by Francisco de Goya from 1808-1812. "Lethe" refers to the River Lethe, which in Greek mythology is one of five rivers of the underworld of Hades. Lethe is personified throughout the Blinded Bulls cycle as an agent of oblivion. *See also 'Lethe' and 'Blinded Bulls' under Recurring Motifs and Symbols.*

Pale Thunder (p.121)
References are made here to the Italian Rennaisance poet Dante Alighieri, Shakespeare's play 'Macbeth', Pieter Breughel and George W Bush (American President). "where crept Lethe in fields of dark / Through the shadows of Bush's hands" refers to the 2003 American invasion of Iraq, where Lethe, the spirit of Oblivion, is given agency through the directives of the then American President George W Bush. *See also 'Lethe' and 'Breughel' under Recurring Motifs and Symbols.*

Landmines (p.124)
"Poussin's Grecian intervention" refers to a painting by Jacque Louis David titled 'The intervention of the Sabine Women' (1799), incorrectly attributed in the poem to Nicolas Poussin, who painted an earlier variation of this theme titled 'The Abduction of the Sabine Women' (1634-1635). Within the logic of the poem Palestine and Israel are personified as "sisters", hence the "inversion of the genders" in regards to their continual conflict. *See also 'Wounded Child' under Recurring Motifs and Symbols.*

Oppenheimer's Score (p.125)
"Julius Robert Oppenheimer (1904 –1967) was an American theoretical physicist and professor of physics at the University of California, Berkeley. Oppenheimer was the wartime head of the Los Alamos Laboratory and is among those who are credited with being the "father of the atomic bomb" for their role in the Manhattan Project, the World War II undertaking that developed the first nuclear weapons." (Wikipedia).

Days Eternal (p.126)
The phrase "Wolund Kiefer's song" is a compression of an artwork title, 'Wolund's Song (with wing)' and the name of its creator, the artist Anselm Kiefer. See also *Kiefer's Song* (p.104), *and 'Blinded Bulls' under Recurring Motifs and Symbols.*

Warning (p.127)
Reference is made here to the American abstract expressionist painter Jackson Pollock (1912-1956), who died in an alcohol related car accident, having struggled with alcoholism all of his life. The lines, "In dances frayed and dangerous / As loose wires in the rain" refer to his action painting technique, where a level of chaos is held spell-bindingly together, but only just. See also 'bronze' in Recurring Motifs and Symbols.

Monstrous Wire (p.128)
See 'Screeching Banshee', 'Dogs', 'Balthus' ball of wool' and 'Mythic square' under Recurring Motifs and Symbols.

Untouched (p.129)
"Rubens' / Furia del pennello" refers to the Flemish painter Peter Paul Rubens, who was said to paint with "furia del pennello", translated as "the fury of the brush." See also 'Dogs' under Recurring Motifs and Symbols.

Songs Unfathomable (p.130)
References are made here to the poets Osip Mandelstam (20th century Russian) and Dante Alighieri (14th century Italian). The lines "...swallows of fire / Arcing from Mandelstam's verse", invoke the image of the swallow in Mandelstam's poetry, transposed in this poem to "Dante's heat", referring to Dante's 14th century poem 'The Inferno'. See also *Pale Thunder* (p.121), *For Osip* (p.78), *Chambers of Autumn Fire* (p.47).

Lorca's Guitar (p.131)
Lorca refers to the Spanish poet and playwright, Federico Garcia Lorca (1898-1936). "Lorca's guitar" alludes to Lorca's 'Poem of the Deep Song' and 'Gypsy Ballads', and the poet's celebration of Andalusian Gypsy culture. Playing the 'guitar' can be seen here as a metaphor for writing poetry.

Blinded Lethe (p.133)
See 'Lethe', 'Bronze' and 'Wounded child' under Recurring Motifs and Symbols.

Ships (p.134)
See 'Blinded bulls', 'Bronze' and 'Ships' under Recurring Motifs and Symbols.

Albatross (p.136)
Reference is made here to Samuel Taylor Coleridge's epic poem 'The Rime of the Ancient Mariner" (1798), where-in an albatross guides the 'Mariner's' ship out of danger, only to be later shot down by the Mariner. The bird, here, can be seen as a guide to the poet and also a personification of tragedy. *See also 'Lethe', 'Birds' and 'Ships' under Recurring Motifs and Symbols.*

Pale Gold (p.138)
The lines "Is scaling the surrendered trophe / Of a fishing ladder / Chagall would understand / The reason for blazing fish / Which flew in Balthus' mind" are rather dense; they refer to two paintings: 'Golgotha' by Marc Chagall (1912) and 'The Cat of La Méditerranée' by Balthus (1949). The surreal nature of the latter painting, featuring a rainbow of flying fish landing on a cat-person's dinner plate is compressed, in the poem, with the multi-coloured ladder in Chagall's painting. Taken together they can be seen as a symbol of enchantment. *See also 'Balthus' cats' and 'Blinded bulls' under Recurring Motifs and Symbols.*

Vision (p.141)
"Samuel's albatross" refers to the albatross in Samuel Taylor Coleridge's epic poem 'The Rime of the Ancient Mariner". See also *Albatross* (p.136). The image of the bird is compressed, in the poem, with the image of "Andrei's tattered skins", referring to a primitive flying aparatus, which features in the opening scenes of Andrei Tarkovsky's film 'Andrei Rublev'.

Together they can be seen as a symbol of creative/spiritual aspiration. *See also Dust (p.54) and 'Birds' under Recurring Motifs and Symbols.*

In The Libraries Of Night (p.143)
Reference is made to Franscisco Goya (1746-1828), and by inference, to his etching suite 'The Disasters of War'. *See also 'Blinded Bulls', 'Gold' and 'Minotaur' under Recurring Motifs and Symbols.*

Lethe's Shadow (p.144)
See 'Wounded Child', 'Gold', 'Blinded Bulls' 'Tunji Beier's Tips' and 'Lethe' under Recurring Motifs and Symbols.

Tips of Fire (p.145)
See 'Tunji Beier's Tips', 'Minotaur' and 'Wounded Child' under Recurring Motifs and Symbols.

Tales of the Mirror (pp.146-152)
The 'Wounded Child', symbolising Suffering leads the blind 'Minotaur', symbolising Creativity through a labyrinth of mirrors. Ultimately the gaze of Suffering and Creativity are one ("the eyes of the Minotaur / In the sockets of the child"). "A mountain from Attar's verse" refers to the Holy mountain of Kaf in Attar's 13th century spiritual classic 'The Conference of the Birds'. The mountain is compressed here with "Billy Goat Hill", a sacred Indigenous site in Alice Springs, Australia. *See also 'Wounded Child', 'Minotaur', 'Balthus's ball of wool', 'Farīd ud-Dīn Attar' and 'Gold' under Recurring Motifs and Symbols.*

Recurring Motifs and Symbols

Balthus' ball of colour/wool: The image invokes the work of the French/Polish painter Balthus, who often depicted cats within his compositions. The popular image of a cat playing with a ball of wool is here conflated with the colours of the paint box. In later poems "Balthus' ball of wool" becomes a symbol for art itself. See the following: *Chambers of Autumn Fire* (p.49), *The Magic Cat is Singing* (p.64), *Surrender* (p.73), *The Pieces Fall* (p.96), *Arrangement* (p.97), *Fists of Now* (p.110), *Monstrous Wire* (p.128), *Pale Gold* (p.138), *Tales of the Mirror* (VIII & X: p. 151).

Balthus' cat 'Balthus' cat' represents the mystery of play, a vital component of any creative act. Found in poems stated above.

Birds Birds are invoked throughout 'Insomnia's Gates' variously as signifiers of innocence, play, spiritual aspiration and guidance. They are often connected to "Attar's birds" (see *Farīd ud-Dīn Attar*), or "Samuel's albatross", referring to the albatross in Samuel Taylor Coleridge's poem, *The Rime of the Ancient Mariner*, which guides the Mariner safely out of Arctic ice. Found in: *Impotence* (p.24), *Glazes on the Highway* (p.35), *Dust* (p.54), *Uncovered* (p.67), *Gentle Blue* (p.68), *Offering* (p.70) *The Black Dog* (p.107), *Albatross* (p.136), *Vision* (p.151).

Blackened Tree The 'black / blackened tree' first appears in *Child* (p.72): "As stories from a black tree / Hidden in the desert". It then re-emerges in *The Tree of Alchemy* (p.113), *Landmines* (p.124) and *Tales of the Mirror* (p.146), signifying, perhaps, the Tree of Life which has been scorched by war.

Blinded Bulls The image first appears in *Uncovered* (p.67) as an oblique reference to Picasso's etching Minotauromachy, which portrays a blind minotaur being led by a girl with a candle. It then reappears in the title poem of the 'Blinded Bulls' cycle (p.115), where the figures in Picasso's etching make a poetic entrance: "The blinded bull has walked into the square / Led by Love". The image, from here on aquires a terrifying aspect, a symbol/agent of relentless terror and chaos. The figure of the minotaur emerges through the cycle as a seperate, though linked, figure to the bulls. Found in: *Uncovered* (p.67), *Blinded Bulls* (p.115), *Thunder* (p.117), *Insomniacs of Nature* (p.120), *On Picasso* (p.122), *Gold Rain* (p.123), *Days Eternal* (p.126), *Ships* (p.134), *Gone* (p.135), *Pale Gold* (p.138), *In the Libraries of Night* (p.143), *Lethe's Shadow* (p.144).

Breughel The Flemish painter, Pieter Breughel the Elder, is invoked as the creator of 'Dulle Griet', his painting from 1563 which depicts Dulle Griet, a figure from Flemish follore (translated as Mad Meg) leading an army of women to pillage hell (see cover image). Traditionally held as a medieval allegory about "noisy, boisterous and covetous women" (wikipedia), the author has always seen it as an ironic image, where the 'mad' one, Griet, is in fact a bastion of sanity, armed and armoured, carrying food and wealth through a world full of war and chaos. Found in: *A Rain of Blood* (p.114), *Pale Thunder* (p.121) and front cover.

Bronze The image of bronze is often employed to conjure a sense of stability, strength and steadfastness, paticularly in the face of danger. Found in: *Faithless* (p.87), *Kiefer's Song* (p.104), *Warning* (p.127), *Blinded Lethe* (p.133), *Ships* (p.134).

Dogs The black dog, or hound is cast as the free spirit of nature. Found in: *Child of the Hunt* (p.18), *Witness* (p.25), *Sleep* (p.44), *Dust* (p.54), *Rings of Blue* (p.72), *Faithless* (p.77), *Pastoral* (p.90), *Promise* (p.98), *Reflections* (p.105), *The Black Dog* (p.107), *The Dogs of Midnight* (p.116), *Warning* (p.127), *Monstrous Wire* (p.128), *Untouched* (p.129).

Farīd ud-Dīn Attar The 13th century mystic poet is invoked on numerous occasions as a signifyer of spiritual/creative freedom/aspiration/conveyance. Many poems reference, in particular 'Attar's birds' which refers to the birds who search for their king (God) on the Mountain of Kaf, in his spiritual classic 'The Conference of the Birds". Found in: *Chambers of Autumn Fire* (p.49), *Dust* (p.54), *Uncovered* (p.67), *Offering* (p.70), *Tales of the Mirror XI* (p.152).

Gold "cases of gold" refers to the background of gold leaf employed in icon painting, which symbolises the spiritual dimension of uncreated light. The use of 'gold' on its own intimates spiritual wealth.

Lethe "Lethe was one of the five rivers of the underworld of Hades. Also known as the Ameles potamos (river of unmindfulness), the Lethe flowed around the cave of Hypnos and through the Underworld where all those who drank from it experienced complete forgetfulness. Lethe was also the name of the Greek spirit of forgetfulness and oblivion, with whom the river was often identified" (Wikipedia). Lethe is personified throughout the 'Blinded Bulls' cycle as an active agent of oblivion.

Minotaur A menacing figure in Greek mythology, the minotaur in 'Blinded Bulls' comes to personify tragic and creativite agency. He first appears as a "blinded bull" in *Blinded Bulls* (p.115): "The Blinded Bull has walked into the square / Led by Love", as an explicit evocation of Picasso's etching 'Minotauromachy' (1934). He then emerges in *Minotaur* (p.128), *In the Libraries of Night* (p.143) and *Tips of Fire* (p.145) as a character distinct from 'the bulls'. In *Tales of the Mirror* (pp.146-152) the Wounded Child and the Minotaur are bound together, as Suffering and Creativity; in the poem the former must lead the latter through the labyrinth inorder for both to achieve transformation.

Mythic square The image is employed throughout 'Insomnia's Gates' as a kind of textual stage, an emblem for the linguistic space of the poem into which various word-agents or characters step.

Rings of blue A deeply mysterious and spiritual image which permeates the 'Rings of Blue' cycle; it intimates a protective ring of sorrowful beauty and spiritual light.

Screeching Banshee "The screeching banshee" refers to a roller door, apparently never oiled, which was below the author's studio when he lived in Melbourne in 2005.

Ships Ships often symbolise a spiritual/creative journey. Found in: *Ships* (p.134), *Albatross* (p.136).

Tunji Beier's tips Tunji Beier (b.1970) is an outstanding world percussionist, whose beats and rhythms have echoed their way into many of the poems in the 'Insomnia's Gates' triology. 'Tunji Beier's tips' refers to the trummel of Beier's fingertips on the various instruments he plays. The memory of Beier's rhythms are invoked to embody a dramatic rise in poetic beat and temperature commensurate with the subject of the given poem. Found in: *Song of the Tavil* (p.23), *Tunji and Fernando* (p.63), *Uncovered* (p.67), *Blinded Bulls* (p.115), *Thunder* (p.117), *Tips of Fire* (p.145).

Wounded Child The Wounded Child is an important archetype, featuring prominently throughout the 'Insomnia's Gates' triology and taking on a heightened significance in the Blinded Bulls cycle. The Child first appears in *Haze* (p.16) as an anonymous child of war. The Child next appears in *Child* (p.74) and *Faithless* (p.77); both poems mark a radical transformation: "he" is now a child-angel with a "broken wing" and an "oil stained shoulder" with "feet of bronze". This transformation reaches its terrifying apotheosis in *Landmines* (p.124), *Blinded Lethe* (p.133) and *Lethe's Shadow* (p.144).

A second Wounded Child figure also appears as a "she" in 'Blinded Bulls'; "she" is the Minotaur's guide, a role borrowed from Picasso's 1934 etching 'Minotauromachy' where a girl with a candle leads a blind minotaur. The Wounded Child as guide appears in *Blinded Bulls* (p.115), *Tips of Fire* (p.145) and *Tales of the Mirror* (pp.146-152). In *Tales of the Mirror* the Wounded Child and the Minotaur are bound together, as Suffering and Creativity; in the poem the former must lead the latter through the labyrinth inorder for both to achieve transformation.

Printed in Great Britain
by Amazon